Ann Boleyn
The Queens Consort
Operetta in three acts
Libretto
Words and Music composed by: Kristina Howells

*****
Ann Boleyn
The Queens Consort
*****

Operetta by Kristina Howells

Ann Boleyn joins the Royal Court of King Henry VIII and Queen Catherine of Aragon. The King immediately takes a fancy to her and attempts to make Ann his new Queen. He successfully manages to divorce Catherine of Aragon and then marries her.

After falling out of favour with Ann, he then finds ways to plot against her and has her tried for incest, witchcraft and adultery, to which she was convicted of. She then finds her last days in the tower, before her execution.

About the Composer

Kristina Howells originally from Dunstable, Great Britain, has dedicated her life to music, and writing. She began her musical studies at the Junior Guildhall School of Music and Drama where she studied, voice and piano, as well as composition, before obtaining her degree at Brunel University London, and Post Graduate Certificate of Music Education at Middlesex University London.

Following her studies she has written a large collection of books, both fiction and nonfiction. She has had two poetry collections published and several songs that she has written, including instrumental pieces. Her orchestral work Calm was accepted by the Royal Philharmonic Orchestra new composer's workshop in 2001 Nottingham that was performed as part of the East Midlands COMA workshops to which she was a member of.

Ann Boleyn is her first ever operetta that she has both written and composed, aided by Frédéric Bara. Her childhood dream of composing her first operetta has finally become a reality.

Her musical works include :
Calm
Secret and Lies
Pride and Prejudice Suite
Collection of Songs
Suite for Piano and Viola
Calm
Violin Concerto
Metamorphose
Psalm 54 SATB

The Story of the Operetta

Act One

Ann Boleyn joins the Royal Court and meets King Henry VIII. During the first meeting he tries to seduce her, and arranges to meet her in the palace gardens. Ann agrees and a love affair starts to evolve. King Henry demands Catherine of Aragon for a divorce and she writes to the Pope asking for his permission, to which was agreed.

Act Two

The King meets Ann Boleyn's parents and asks for their permission to marry their daughter. They refuse to give their permission; Ann and the King elope to France and marry in Calais, before celebrating the wedding at the palace upon their return. Ann tells Henry upon returning from France that she is pregnant and she gives birth to a daughter. The King is not happy, he has a daughter as an heir to the throne and problems in their marriage start to occur.

Act Three

The King has a private council meeting to find out if the rumours he has heard are true about Ann's infidelity. The members of the council agree that they are and she is then tried under the act of treason. She is convicted and sentenced to death. She finishes her last days in the tower of London, hoping for a Royal pardon, which never came.

Roles

Ann Boleyn
King Henry VIII
Catherine of Aragon
Lady Elizabeth Howard
Thomas Boleyn
Priest
Thomas Howard
Henry Percy
Judge
Servant
Chorus – jesters, jury, members of the court, soldiers

Index

Act I

Scene I

(In the Royal Court).

No 1 Choir

Hail the King
Hail the King
As he arrives with his Queen
Catherine

Let's all stand
Let's all stand
In honour of the
King and Queen

See the jesters
See the jesters
Watch how they perform
Before the King

The musicians play
The musicians play
The Kings favourite air
See how they play

Hail the King
Hail the King
As he arrives with his Queen
Catherine

(Jesters do their acts; dancers dance a gavotte before the King and Queen)

Instrumental Music - Gavotte

Text One

Ann: Your Royal Highness I am here at your service.

Catherine: Ah Henry may I introduce you to my new maid of honour. She is of fine breeding.

Henry: The pleasure is all mine. What is your name?

Ann: My name is Ann. (*Courtesy's before the King*).

No 2 Duet King Henry and Ann Boleyn

Ann: I am your lady in waiting
Experienced as I am
A daughter of a diplomat
Here I am

I am here at your service
I do all that you ask
My mother is the daughter
Of the Duke of Norfolk

I am happy to be here
Amongst your fine court
Returning from the courts in France
I can speak French

I am your lady in waiting
Experienced as I am
A daughter of a diplomat
Here I am

(King gets up and goes towards her, taking her hand).

Henry: My dear Ann
How nice to meet you
You are a beautiful one
I truly find

So nice to have you
Here in the court
I will make you happy
Meet me tomorrow

I want to see you
You will find me alone
In the palace gardens
Beside the statue

Henry:	Please say you will
	I want you for mine
	My wife I will divorce
	So you can be mine

(The king and Ann dance a gavotte)

Text Two

Henry:	Say you will meet me.
Anne	I really don't know your Royal Majesty
Henry:	My servants will come to find you.
Ann:	You know your Royal Majesty.
Henry:	Please Henry (he interrupts).
Ann:	Henry, you are married.
Henry:	It is of no importance, meet me tomorrow, and I will tell you all. I want to see you my beautiful Ann.

(The King rejoins Catherine of Aragon. Anne takes her place next to her.)

Hail the King
Hail the King
As he arrives with his Queen
Catherine

Let's all stand
Let's all stand
In honour of the
King and Queen

See the jesters
See the jesters
Watch how they perform
Before the King

The musicians play
The musicians play
The Kings favourite air
See how they play

Hail the King
Hail the King
As he arrives with his Queen
Catherine

(Jesters do their acts; dancers dance a gavotte before the King and Queen)

Instrumental Music

(Black out – leaving Ann alone)

No 3 Ann's Air

Ann: 1.

Oh what folie
Does await
What have I done?
To merit such a fate

Chorus:

Oh what folie
Oh what joy?
Oh what folie
Oh what joy?

2.

Oh what folie
My heart is in two
What will I do?
Not to make foe

Chorus:

Oh what folie
Oh what joy?
Oh what folie
Oh what joy?

3.

Oh what folie
The King has shown
I know not
For my love is unknown

Chorus:

Oh what folie
Oh what joy?
Oh what folie
Oh what joy?

4.

Oh what folie
That awaits
Tomorrow is the day
My fate awaits

Chorus:

Oh what folie
Oh what joy?
Oh what folie
Oh what joy?

5.   Oh what folie
            In the garden
            I will find
            With my king

Chorus: Oh what folie
            Oh what joy?
            Oh what folie
            Oh what joy?
            Oh what folie
            Oh what joy?
            Oh what folie
            Oh what joy?

            (End of scene one)

Scene II

(Ann's bedroom)

(Ann is alone in her bedroom, a servant knocks on the door and Ann opens it.)

Text Three

Servant: A letter for you Miss Ann.

(The servant hands the letter to Ann and then leaves.)

Ann: Thank you.

(Ann takes the letter and starts to read it.)

Dearest Ann, how nice it was to meet you yesterday. I've been unable to sleep. I'm looking forward to seeing you, my dearest one. Meet me in the palace gardens by the fountain. There I will be waiting for you. Love your Henry.

Ann: Oh what folie
        What shall I do?
        What will happen?
        I do not know

        Oh how I worry
        What lies ahead?
        With the King
        The King of England

        Oh what folie
        Such decisions
        My heart is beating
        I know not why?

        I have no choice
        I have to go
        To meet my King
        By the statue

        Oh what folie
        That I now find
        In the arms of a King
        In an hour's time

        (Ann sits down, breaths deeply and looks in the mirror).

Text four

Ann: What have I done coming here? It was seen as a golden opportunity to work
          with the Queen of England. Oh how I feel I am betraying her. Her loyal servant
          about to get with her King! A king, so powerful and overwhelming, charms me
          with this letter, a letter and words of undying affection. Oh how my heart
          melts, as I await to see him.

Ann: Oh what folie
          What shall I do?
          What will happen?
          I do not know

          Oh how I worry
          What lies ahead?
          With the King
          The King of England

          Oh what folie
          That I now find
          In the arms of a King
          In an hour's time

                    (Servant knocks at the door).

Text five

Servant: The king is waiting Miss Ann, please follow me.

(Ann exists with the servant and leaves for the palace gardens).

End of Scene II

Scene III

(The king is standing beside the statue – Ann joins him).

Text Six

Henry: My darling Ann how lovely it is to see you. (*He takes her hand*).

Ann: The pleasure is all mine.

Henry: I could not sleep my dearest one. Your angelic face was on my mind. Your smiles, your voice, my dearest Ann, say you will be mine.

Ann: Henry, we do not know each other. What words you say? How am I to resist you, my King?

Henry: My darling Ann, I've written you a song. Would you like to hear it?

Ann: Of course if it pleases you Henry.

Henry: Then I shall sing it.

No 5 Henry's Air
Greensleeves

Henry: 1.   Alas my love
                          You do me wrong
                          To cast me off discourteously
                          And I have loved you so long
                          Delighting in your company

             Chorus: Greensleeves was all my joy
                          Greensleeves was my delight
                          Greensleeves was my heart of gold
                          And who but my Lady Greensleeves

             2.   If you intend thus to disdain
                          It does the more enrapture me
                          And even so,
                          I still remain a lover in captivity

             Chorus: Greensleeves was all my joy
                          Greensleeves was my delight
                          Greensleeves was my heart of gold
                          And who but my Lady Greensleeves

(Henry takes Ann by the hand and looks into her eyes.)

Text Seven

Henry: My dearest Ann, say that you will be mine.

Ann: My dear Henry, how you do me so well. But you are married.

Henry: My heart no longer loves Catherine. She gives me no heirs. I have no longer a
           real need for her. I do not love her. It is you I want, my dearest Ann. Oh how I
           love you. And I know that you will love me, as I love you. Say that you will be
           mine.

Ann: I do not know.

Henry: Please Ann I will never leave you alone. I will pursue you until you agree. I
           will divorce Catherine and make you my Queen, my darling Ann.

Ann: Oh how I am confused
I do not know
My heart starts to beat
For the love of a King

Oh how is this possible?
I really don't know
I never thought that
This would be

Oh how it is
Where is my dearest
How do I reply?
To the King of England

Oh how I am confused
Please God help me
I pray
That I will make the right decision

Text Eight

| Ann: | King Henry, you are so persuasive. How am I to refuse you? If only you will divorce your Queen, then I will accept to be your wife. |
| Henry: | Then if I am to divorce Catherine, so be it. I will prove to you that she will no longer be Queen and I will take you as mine. |

(Henry exits leaving Ann Alone).

Ann: Oh what folie
            What shall I do?
            What will happen?
            I do not know

            Oh how I worry
            What lies ahead?
            With the King
            The King of England

            Oh what folie
            That I now find
            In the arms of a King
            For the rest of my lifetime

                        (End of Scene III)

Scene IV

(Catherine is in her chamber of the castle reading, when the King Henry storms in)

Text Nine

Catherine:	Henry where have you been that makes you so angry?
Henry:	I am not angry.
Catherine:	What is with this attitude? You have been so distant for a few days now. I do not understand.
Henry:	Catherine, I have something to tell you. I want you to listen.

Henry: It has been a while
            I no longer love thee
            Eternity of love
            Does not exist

            I want us to finish
            Say that you agree
            I don't want to hurt you
            My Queen

Catherine: I've known for a while
            I was not going to last
            You are too impulsive
            Love the girls

            Want to sleep with them
            And then in my bed
            I lay, Hurting
            Praying for her King

Henry: I'm so sorry Catherine
            I don't know how
            I can repair this
            I know I've hurt you

            Write a letter
            To the cardinals
            This is what I want
            A divorce

(Musical interlude – Catherine gets up and looks out of the window).

Catherine: Henry darling
            I still love you
            Despite
            Hurting me

            But out of respect
            For King and country
            I will agree
            To a divorce

Henry: Oh how my dear lady
            You do me so well
            My heart is
            Ever yours

            You've given me
            Power to move on
            And for you too
            Thank you my Queen

            (Music plays out as King then exits)

Text ten

Catherine: Oh what have I done? I really don't love the King's ways. I will give him his divorce. I will write to the Pope and all the cardinals on behalf of the King.

(She goes to her bureau and takes out a paper and a quill and starts to write).

Dear Pope, I am writing to you with due regret. I want to divorce the King of England. If you refuse, the King will do all he can to ensure that the Catholic Church is abolished in England. Please I pray you will adhere to the King. If you refuse, your church will no longer exist in England.
Yours truly, Queen Catherine!

(Catherine puts the letter into the envelope, and rings the bell. The servant arrives and takes the letter.)

Musical interlude

Henry: Queen Catherine, thank you. The divorce has been agreed at the Priory in Dunstable. It is the only Priory left standing throughout the entire Kingdom. The Pope has washed his hands off of England. I am now the head of the church. You are now free to go. Farewell my Queen.

(Catherine gets up).

Catherine: Farewell Henry.

(Catherine leaves – blackout).

End of Act One Scene IV

Act II

Scene I

(Outside the home of Ann Boleyn's parents).

Text One

Ann:	Henry darling do not be worried. My parents are not monsters and they won't eat you.
Henry:	My dearest Ann, oh how I feel so nervous.
Ann:	I understand my darling, but you are the King of England. How can they object?

(Ann smiles reassuringly – the door opens).

Lady Elizabeth Howard:	Darling Ann, how nice it is to see you.
Ann:	Mother I have someone to introduce to you, this is Henry.

(Pause).

Lady Elizabeth Howard:	Please enter. Thomas darling, Ann and Henry.

(Thomas gets up and shakes the hand of the King).

Thomas Boleyn:	Nice to meet you.

Henry:

I know not why I have come here
To see you both together
But I have something important
To say
I love Ann and I want to marry her

Without your approval
I do not care
My intentions are honourable
I am the King and I want your daughter
As my Queen

If you do not agree
I do not care
Ann and I
Will run away
And get married, far, far away

I know not why I have come here
To see you both together
But I have something important
To say
I love Ann and I want to marry her

No 2 Quartet, Henry, Ann, Lady Elisabeth Howard, Thomas Boleyn

Lady Elizabeth Howard Thomas Boleyn	If it pleases your Royal Highness How can we refuse? But take our daughter We will not give	
Ann	Mother, Father How can you deny? The King of England His Bride	
Lady Elizabeth Howard Thomas Boleyn	If it pleases your Royal Highness How can we refuse? But take our daughter We will not give	
Lady Elizabeth Howard Thomas Boleyn	If it pleases your Royal Highness How can we refuse? But take our daughter We will not give	Henry: I am the king All is mine I will make Ann My Bride
Ann:	Mother, Father I am sorry to trouble you But I will be Queen of England	

(Henry and Ann exits).

No 3 Duet Lady Elizabeth Howard and Thomas Boleyn

Lady Elizabeth Howard: Oh how stubborn
Is our daughter
To fall in love
In such a manner

Thomas Boleyn: I am afraid
We may never see
Our dearest Ann
In the same way again

Lady Elizabeth Howard: Oh How I am afraid   Thomas Boleyn: I am afraid
Of how her life   without wanting more
Will soon change   We may never see
Together: Our darling daughter Ann

(Black out).

End of Scene I

(Henry and Ann in Calais France)

No 4 Duet Henry and Ann

Ann: My darling Henry
Oh how I feel free
To be with you
For an eternity

I never imagined
My life like this
Soon to be beside you
As your Queen

Henry: My darling Ann
Oh how I am happy
To be with you
For an eternity

I have never imagined
My life like this
Soon to be beside you
As your king

Ann:	My darling Henry	Henry:	My darling Ann
	Oh how I feel free		Oh how I am happy
	To be with you		To be with you
	For an eternity		For an eternity

Text Two

Henry: My darling Ann in less than thirty minutes we are married.

Ann: It's hard to believe that we will soon be one.

Henry: My love for you is so strong. I do not want to hurt you.

Ann: My darling Henry, oh how I am pleased to hear you say such kind words. I can
            hear the bells ringing aloud for us.

Henry: The time has come for us to enter the house of God to wed.

            (Henry takes Ann's hand and they exit – blackout).

(The Priest enters – followed by Henry and Ann)

Text Three

Priest: Dearly beloved we are gathered here today in the sight of God to join together this man and woman in Holy Matrimony. If any man can show any just cause why they may not lawfully be joined together, let him speak, or else hereafter forever hold his peace. If no impediment be alleged, then I say unto King Henry of England wilt though have this woman as thy wedded wife, to live together after God's ordinance in thy Holy state of Matrimony? Wilt thee love her, comfort her, honour and keep her in sickness and health and forsaking all other, keep thee only unto her, so long as ye both shall live?

Henry: I will.

Priest: Ann will you take King Henry of England to be thy wedded husband, to live together after God's ordinance in the Holy state of Matrimony? Wilt thee obey him, and serve him, love, honour, and keep him in sickness and in health, and forsaking all other, keep thee only unto him, so long as ye both shall live?

Ann: I will.

Priest: Then I pronounce you man and wife. You may now kiss the bride.

(Black out during the kiss – change of scenery outside the church – lights up).

42

Ann:	Oh my Henry How I never thought I'd be your wife After so much strife
Henry:	Oh my Ann You make me happy Your beauty and youth You are a part of me
Ann and Henry:	Together we will rule Our love will inspire all Together we will rule The great Kingdom of England
Ann:	Oh my Henry How happy I am To be your Queen And stay by your side
Henry:	Oh my Ann How happy I am To have you as my Queen And stay by my side
Ann and Henry:	Together we will rule Our love will inspire all Together we will rule The great Kingdom of England

(Black out).

End of Scene II

No 6 Choir

Hail the King
Hail the King
As he arrives with his
New Queen Ann

Let's all stand
Let's all stand
In honour of the
King and Queen

See the jesters
See the jesters
Watch how they perform
Before the King

The musicians play
The musicians play
The Kings favourite air
See how they play

Hail the King
Hail the King
As he arrives with his
New Queen Ann

(Jesters do their acts; dancers dance a gavotte before the King and Queen)

Instrumental Music - Gavotte

Text three

Ann: My dearest Henry I have great news. I am pregnant.

Henry: Oh my darling Ann this is fantastic, let's celebrate.

Henry: Everyone, listen Ann my Queen is pregnant. I am to become a father, and an heir to the throne has been pronounced.

Chorus: Hip, hip, hooray, hip, hip, hooray to the King and Queen of England.

Hail the King
Hail the Queen
As they await
The birth of their child

What great news?
What great news?
Unfolds in the
Royal household

Hail the King
Hail the Queen
As they await
The birth of their child

Oh what joy?
Oh what joy?
We will have
As we await for the baby

Hail the King
Hail the Queen
As we await
For the Royal Heir

End of scene III

(Ann alone with her daughter).

No 8 Ann's Air

Ann: My dearest Elizabeth
          I never thought to have
          You in my arms

          My dearest Elizabeth
          What joy you bring
          Into my life

          My dearest Elizabeth
          I will protect you
          From all harm

          My dearest Elizabeth
          Oh how sad I am
          But happy you are mine

          My dearest Elizabeth
          I never thought to have
          You in my arms

Text four

Henry: Ann I wanted a son and you've given me a daughter.

Ann: I cannot be responsible for the sex of our child.

Henry: I wanted a boy as an heir and not a girl. What will become of the throne?

Ann: It is not my problem Henry. Our baby is beautiful, take a look.

Henry: I do not want to know.

Ann: Oh how cruel you are to an innocent creature what we have created.

No 9 Duet Henry and Ann

Henry: I am the King of England
I do not want
A Queen to dictate
How I should react

Ann: I know my dear
I am not a fool
But she's your daughter
Look at her

Henry: I wanted a son
You gave me a girl
I do not want
This creature

Ann: My Royal Highness
What can I say?
I fear for my life
My Henry dear

Henry: I am the King of England
I do not want
A Queen to dictate
How I should react

(The king storms out)

Ann: Oh what Folie
No more joy
My dearest daughter

May your reign
Be the finest
England ever has

Musical interlude

End of Act II

Act III

(In the King's chamber)

No 1 Henry's Air

Henry: Welcome Gentleman into my office
I am glad to see you
We have a state emergency
The Queen has betrayed me
I know not what to do
As I lay awake
In a state
The Queen
I am afraid
Has betrayed me for another

My dearest council members
We have to act
Tell me all what you can
So I can end this pain
And recreate
A new history
For all to see
As I want to put on trial
The Queen
For betraying me

Text One

Thomas Howard:	I am afraid your Royal Majesty, it may be true.
Henry Purcell:	Reports are circulating around the country that Ann may have in fact had an affair.
Thomas Howard:	The many miscarriages that she has had could be the result of an undying yearning for another elsewhere.
Henry Purcell:	Another man perhaps has captured her heart, or she is bewitched by a peasant from afar.
Henry:	So many questions I know not. Tell me more, I want to know.

No 2 Duet Thomas Howard and Henry Percy

Thomas Howard: Messengers
                  That we are
                  Have been called
                  From afar

Henry Percy: To deal with
                  The kings private
                  State of affairs
                  Concerning love and hate

Together: Your Royal Majesty
                  The news is not good
                  We are afraid
                  You've been misunderstood

Thomas Howard: Witchcraft
                  Could
                  Have been
                  All but the cause

Henry Percy: Or adultery and incest
                  Is only
                  That of
                  The devils curse

Together: Your Royal Majesty
                  The news is not good
                  We are afraid
                  You've been misunderstood

Text Two

Henry:	Gentlemen I no longer want to hear. The decision I want to take is of this. Thomas, can you organise the judge to take on the case? To put the Queen on trial, for witchcraft, adultery and incest!
Thomas Howard:	Of course your majesty. It will be a pleasure to see the Queen in the tower.
Henry Percy:	I must confess we have witnesses who can all agree to these things we have presented to thee.
Henry:	Then go ahead, and leave me to be. I need to rest, as I order soldiers to arrest the Queen.

(Henry Percy and Thomas Howard leave the King alone).

Henry: Oh what folie
           Oh what a nightmare
           Oh what folie
           Oh what a nightmare

           What has become
           Of my mind
           How can the Queen?
           Be cursed and so unkind

           Oh what folie
           Oh what a nightmare
           Oh what folie
           Oh what a nightmare

           The day we married
           The happiest occasion it was
           Now to death
           And to destruction

           Oh what folie
           Oh what a nightmare
           Oh what folie
           Oh what a nightmare

(The King leaves).

End of Scene I

Scene II

(In the court house).

Text Three

Judge: Please will the court rise for the King of England.

Judge: The following charges
Have been bought
Amongst Queen Ann Boleyn
And the state

The truth must be heard
The court awaits
To hear of what
Will become of the state

What we are to hear
Is not a cry
Not a tear
As death is nigh

The truth must be heard
The court awaits
To hear of what
Will become of the state

Text Four

Judge:	The King of England versus the Queen of England let the case begin. The court calls Henry Percy to take to the stand. You are to tell the truth, the whole truth and nothing but the truth, so be to God.

Henry Percy: My name is Henry Percy. I was a boyfriend of Ann Boleyn. We met when we were very young. We got married. The marriage was annulled by the Cardinal Thomas Wolsey as not being of fine standing. The marriage never took place. Yet it could be said, it was consumed. Ann left for France, and I know that she is very loyal. It is hard to believe that she could have had another when she was with me. This was not the case as she loved me entirely.

Judge: Thank you, now the court calls Thomas Boleyn to take to the stand. You are to tell the truth, the whole truth and nothing but the truth, so be to God.

Thomas Boleyn: My name is Thomas Boleyn. I am the father of Ann Boleyn. My daughter during her marriage to the King has been seen by servants to have had affairs in secret, including that of her own brother Lord George Rochford. She has had meetings with a woman peasant close to our home. We never knew why. We saw strange objects flying by. Ann I thought, I thought I knew my daughter. It is a shame. This has had to pass. To save the throne of England, her fate must take priority as the court decides.

Judge: Thank you, now the court calls Queen of England Ann Boleyn to take to the stand. You are to tell the truth, the whole truth, and nothing but the truth, so be to God.

Ann: This is what I want to say. I want my voice to be heard. I am not of what you think! My fate awaits that I know. My father has told you of what I am to say are lies. Please I know you will do what is right. Let me say one thing to the King. You have chosen me from low estate to be your Queen and companion, far beyond my desert or desire. If then you found me worthy of such honour, good your grace, let not any light fancy or bad counsel of my enemies withdraw your princely favour from me. Neither let their stain that unworthy stain of a disloyal heart towards your good grace ever cast so foul a plot on me, and on the infant princess your daughter.

59

(Ann breaks down and cries).

Judge: The jury you have heard. It is up to you to decide. The Queen's life is in your hands, but also the future of England too. Take into consideration of what you have to do?

Jury Member: The jury needs not to deliberate, we all agree guilty of treason to the state.

Guilty as charged
Guilty as charged
Queen Ann Boleyn
Guilty as charged

We've heard the case
We've heard the case
Queen Ann Boleyn
We've heard the case

To the gallows
To the gallows
Queen Ann Boleyn
To the gallows

Death in the tower
Death in the tower
Queen Ann Boleyn
Death in the tower

Chopping off the head
Chopping off the head
Queen Ann Boleyn
Chopping off the head

In a public execution
In a public execution
Queen Ann Boleyn
A public execution

Guilty as charged
Guilty as charged
Queen Ann Boleyn
Guilty as charged

Text Five

Judge:

The court's decision has been made. Queen Ann Boleyn of England you are to die for treason to the state, as you are guilty of the following crimes, incest, adultery and witchcraft. Now take her to the tower!

(Ann is led out)

Chorus:

Hooray, the Queen is to die, Hooray.

End of Scene II

Scene III

(In the Tower)
(Ann writes a letter to Henry).

Text Six

Ann: Dearest Henry oh how I wish, things were different. I bought into the world our beautiful daughter Elizabeth. Please look after her. Oh how I am sad for our daughter to lose her mother. May God protect you both, as I await for the executioners to take me to the gallows, your beloved Ann.

Ann: My life is almost at an end
There is no more hope for me
I really love
The King, King Henry

How could it all have got so bad?
I gave him a
Beautiful daughter
There was never another man

Oh how evil men had plot
Against me and all that I am
I am too weak to hate
God forgive them for they know not

My life is almost at an end
There is no more hope for me
I really love
The King, King Henry

Text Seven

Ann: I am come hither to die, for according to the law and by the law I am judged to die, and therefore I will speak nothing against it. I am come hither to accuse no man, nor to speak anything of that. Where I am accused and condemned to die, but I pray God save the King and send him long to reign over you.

(Ann is led out of the tower).

Instrumental Music

End of Act III